CREATED FOR MORE

by LACEY WHITTAKER

Edited by Lil Barcaski and Justin Whittaker

Published by: GWN Publishing
www.GWNPublishing.com

Cover Design: Kristina Conatser | Captured by KC Designs
www.CapturedbyKCDesigns.com

ISBN: 978-1-959608-04-2

INTRODUCTION

Ephesians 2:10

Heart set on Him. Do not rely on your own understanding. Trust in Him all of your days. He will direct your steps. Never forget your praise. Surrender. Smile. Conquer all things. You were created for more. That's our faith.

"For we are His workmanship [His own master work, a work of art], created in Christ Jesus [reborn from above—spiritually transformed, renewed, ready to be used] for good works, which God prepared [for us] beforehand [taking paths which He set], so that we would walk in them [living the good life which He prearranged and made ready for us]."

Ephesians 2:10 AMP

We are created for more. For more than our minds could ever imagine. We are open vessels. We are blessed by the God who created us to do good works long before we were born. He has prepared the ones that accept and hold this scripture in their hands. He has prepared. Will you be a part of His plan?

His workmanship, handiworks, masterpiece. Yes, you are His masterpiece. You have been created by God. You have. There is not another in this whole world like you. God has created you to be the only you here. He has created you for a relationship with Him. To abide in Him and bear good fruits. He has created you as you. Thank Him today. There is not another like you.

When you commit your life to Him. When you believe He is who He says He is. When you proclaim Jesus is the only way to heaven. This is the key. The key you walk in, being created for more than this world sees. It's heaven's keys to the Kingdom. Yes, you hold them as you are now reborn in spirit by Him. Walk a new life. Don't look back. You have been created to truly live, at last.

You are ready to be used. Walk the good path in faith. Bow down as He creates. He gives life to the fullest when you surrender and see it as good. Not your will, but His. Pleasing Him is part of His mighty plan. He knows best. He knows rest. Follow Him, and see the everlasting victory He has given for you and me.

"You are worthy, our Lord and God, to receive glory, honor, and power, for You created all things, and for Your pleasure they were created and exist."

Revelation 4:11 TPT

You created us to exist. For Your pleasure. You created us. I can't fathom this. I can't fathom why. You are worthy and to be praised, to be exalted over any other name. You are worthy, it's true, all the glory and honor to You. All my days, I shall proclaim You are Lord over my name.

"But from the beginning of the creation, God 'made them male and female.'

Mark 10:6 NKJV

You created your sons and daughters. You created male and female. You created us to love one another in sickness and health. You created us to be well.

"Praise the one who created every heavenly light! His tender love for us continues on forever!"

Psalms 136:7 TPT

You created us to love. To show love, be love, and have love. Love is the key. You created us, with love, to see. Love conquers all things.

"The Lord formed me from the beginning, before He created anything else."

Proverbs 8:22 NLT

To be thought of first. He created us first. Oh, how it is to be first in His eyes. To always be the very best prize. Oh, the first He created, He created so well. Lord in Heaven, let You always be first in the story I tell.

"The rich and the poor have this in common, The Lord is the maker of them all."

Proverbs 22:2 NKJV

We were all created. The rich and the poor, He created them all. The humble and pure. The large mockery of this world. He created us all. So, love one another at all costs. He has created us all, so love one another as He bore the cross in love. His blood poured out, now there is no doubt. We were created to love.

"Remember how short my time is; For what futility have You created all the children of men?"

Psalms 89:47 NKJV

Our time is short here. Live like you are fully created for more. For more will be soon here at heaven's door. More will be here soon. More, oh more, will be. Honor Him with your everlasting surrender and peace He shall give to you all of your days. Living as He created, set on His way.

"My frame was not hidden from You, When I was made in secret, And skillfully wrought in the lowest parts of the earth."

Psalms 139:15 NKJV

May we never forget it was You that formed us in our mother's womb. You knitted us together for perfection in Your sight. Your hand was on us, and our paths were clear to You before we entered this world. Help us live, created for more.

"You saw who You created me to be, before I became me! Before I'd ever seen the light of day, the number of days You planned for me were already recorded in Your book."

Psalms 139:16 TPT

Our days are numbered as we read. Our days, our lives, we owe to Thee. We owe them, Father, only to You. Help us to live these days honoring You. Never let a day pass without a surrender that will always last.

"So we are convinced that every detail of our lives is continually woven together for good, for we are His lovers who have been called to fulfill His designed purpose."

Romans 8:28 TPT

Be convinced that we were made for purpose. Be intent, and love Him for it. Be intent, He created you to live, truly, only for Him. Every detail of our lives, you see, doesn't come from you or me. It comes from our God who sees everything.

"and have put on the new [spiritual] self who is being continually renewed in true knowledge in the image of Him who created the new self—"

Colossians 3:10 AMP

Born in the spirit. Being renewed each day. Day by day, be renewed and have knowledge for He created us to know things. He created us to know Him, be like Him, honor and love Him. Knowing Him, obeying Him, and hearing Him. Seek wisdom, and knowledge will be given to you. You were born to live it, it's true.

You were created, born, made, designed, and prepared for more, greater, higher, mightier ways than your eyes could see. You were created to be His glory, His friend, and His everything. You were created for far more than your ears have heard. Your mind may wander, but still never fully grasp this creation He has created for no small task. He asks for our yes and our belief. Oh, how we were created to believe.

"Behold, God, my salvation! I will trust and not be afraid, For the Lord God is my strength and song; Yes, He has become my salvation."

Isaiah 12:2 AMP

Salvation. Are you saved? Do you deny evil ways? Are you saved? Do you bow down to the King of kings or earthly graves? Are you saved? Do you believe we were bought at a cost? Do you believe sin no longer holds us to death? Do you believe Jesus is the only way? Answer upon today. Confess your sins, repent and ask Him to enter in. Live a life fully for Him. Today, today, today.

We are called to trust. To live a life trusting God. We are to draw our strength from the only one that knows our cause. Trust Him today. Rely on His everlasting grace. His love casts all burdens away. Say you trust Him today.

"Trust in the Lord with all your heart, And lean not on your own understanding;"

Proverbs 3:5 NKJV

Do not seek trust through your eyes or flesh. Seek trust through the Holy Spirit. Seek trust through Him that gives. Seek trust, and rely on His goodness and never changing ways. Seek trust, and obey. Seek trust, and you will find peace. Seek trust, and believe. Seek trust, and never try to understand. Seek trust, and know He always lends His hand.

"Fear not, for I am with you; Be not dismayed, for I am your God. I will strengthen you, Yes, I will help you, I will uphold you with My righteous right hand.'"

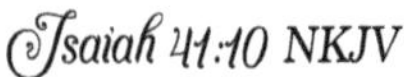

We were not created to live in fear. So, why do we live there often? What causes fear? What strikes you or holds you? What gives you worry? Why is the world full of fear? Listen so clear. Yield to Him, and hear the sweet whispers. He longs to give the smile and the peace. It's all His plan. His nature is to give peace, so why don't you set yourself free? Do not be troubled or dismayed, call on your Father to pull you from the heavy grave.

I am your God; I will strengthen you, He spoke. He spoke this truth. He wants to strengthen you. Will you let Him? Are you open and willing? Are you hoping and feeling? Are you? I look up to the heavens and find my strength. The only way to fully release. Surrender myself and find a new life in You.

When fear hits and your strength is weak, laugh and say, enemy, you are a thief. No longer shall you delay my purpose, my thoughts, or my plans. I am created by a Father that lasts. He lasts and you fade. I proclaim you to leave me alone today. I cast you down, I cast you out. If you choose to stick around, you can sit back and watch me pray, pray, praise.

Flow. What blocks it? What stops it? What keeps it staggering along? Flow. Flow. We were created for a heavenly flow. The Holy Ghost flow. Seek it, live it, watch it wreck all other ways. Watch it grow and sing praise. Watch it abound in higher ways, in that flow, we long to stay.

We were created for the intimate relationship with Him. The one on one. The one that always draws near. Do you long for this? Do you know how to get it? Do you feel His presence often? Do you want to live in it? We are called to. Ask Him today, to show you, His way.

He says follow. He says, follow me. Do you follow Him? Do you want to follow Him? Do you want to give up your own lead to please the God who sees our needs? Do you? Do you want to give up control? Surrender, and see that following Him is the very best thing.

"My sheep hear My voice, and I know them, and they follow Me."

To know His voice. Oh, to really know His voice. To know our shepherd's voice. It's everything. It's key. He leads. We need not to wander, but drown out the noise of this world. He leads. Listen for His voice today. Follow Him and be ok.

"If you want to be my disciple, follow Me, and you will go where I am going. And if you truly follow Me as my disciple, the Father will shower his favor upon your life."

John 12:26 TPT

Yearn to be His disciple. Yearn for that close relationship. Yearn for the path less taken. The narrow road that never will be forsaken. Yearn for this. Watch the favor of His hand upon your life as a faithful servant of the Lord Jesus Christ.

"Then Jesus said to His disciples, "If anyone desires to come after Me, let him deny himself, and take up his cross, and follow Me."

Matthew 16:24 NKJV

Deny yourself. Crucify your flesh. Deny your wants. Deny the evil ways. Deny yourself. Take up His cross. Live freely at all costs. Do not conform to the patterns of this world. Follow Him. Follow Him, and watch how you will soar in His plans.

"And He said to them, "Follow Me [as My disciples, accepting Me as your Master and Teacher and walking the same path of life that I walk], and I will make you fishers of men."

Matthew 4:19 AMP

Walk the path He asks. Walk the path. Accept Him as your master and teacher. Learn His heart. You will no longer be fishers of worldly things, but fishers of men for heaven's kingdom. Take as many with you as you can. This is His path, His purpose for you. This is His plan.

"And then He told them, "Go into all the world and preach the Good News to everyone."

Mark 16:15 NLT

He said go into all the world and preach the good news. Are you? Are you spreading the good news? Are you a light to be seen? Are you loving in all things? Are you praying and giving? Are you serving? Are you obeying this command? Are you lending your hands? Are you? Do you have peace reading this scripture, or are you convicted, left in linger? Ask Him your part today and go out and share His great name!

"But even as Jesus said this, a crowd approached, led by Judas, one of the twelve disciples. Judas walked over to Jesus to greet him with a kiss."

Luke 22:47 NLT

You were created for more. You chose to walk the path He has set, then you meet your Judas. You meet him. He greets you with a kiss. You are devastated. You are betrayed. You are shaken and left for dead. You are at the lowest of lows. You have been struck and cut. You have experienced your deepest blow. Where do you go? Go to Him. He walked this earth and was dealt the very worst. He walked through everything that has ever been done to you. Go to Him. Go to Him, the Father of all. Go to Him and let Him heal your broken heart.

"You can pass through His open gates with the password of praise. Come right into His presence with thanksgiving. Come, bring your thank offering to Him, and affectionately bless is beautiful name!"

We were created for worship. We are to worship Him with everything we have. We are to worship Him with our mind, body, soul, and spirit. Will you choose to worship Him with your everything today?

"Bless and praise the Lord, you mighty warriors,
ministers who serve him well and fulfill his desires."

Psalms 103:21 TPT

We are called to serve Him. His desire is for us to serve Him and be a good and faithful servant. I want to leave this life here, hearing well done, good and faithful servant.

"Do nothing from selfishness or empty conceit [through factional motives, or strife], but with [an attitude of] humility [being neither arrogant nor self-righteous], regard others as more important than yourselves."

Philippians 2:3 AMP

Be humble. Go low. Let others a rise. Go low. Be humble. He asks these of us. To think of others as more important than ourselves. Let pride die. Be humble. Be secure. Be lowly, He sees where He calls us to be. He sees. Be humble. Be free.

"But He continues to pour out more and more grace upon us. For it says, "God resists you when you are proud, but continually pours out grace when you are humble."

James (Jacob) 4:6 TPT

Be humble, and watch grace overflow upon your soul. Grace, upon grace, upon grace. He saves. Grace, upon grace, upon grace. Grace, mercy, kindness you shall receive.

"For Yahweh is always good and ready to receive you. He's so loving that it will amaze you— so kind that it will astound you! And he is famous for his faithfulness toward all. Everyone knows our God can be trusted, for He keeps His promises to every generation!"

Psalms 100:5 TPT

He is always good. Always good. Look up. Look up to Him. Look up and receive. He is always good. He is always very good. Always. Nothing could ever change His faithful ways of being good to us. Nothing could change this. Nothing. He is always so good. Receive His goodness today. Receive it. Believe it.

"And then He will send His angels, and gather together His elect from the four winds, from the farthest part of earth to the farthest part of heaven."

Mark 13:27 NKJV

On the final day, I want to be gathered. I want to be the chosen. I want to be. I want to be gathered His way. My faith. His way. I pray to be gathered. I pray all will be gathered that day. I pray.

"Have I really become your enemy because I tell you the truth?"

Galatians 4:16 TPT

You are created to be a truth teller. Truth, authentic, honesty, realness. Being a truth teller could make you an enemy of this world. It will make you an enemy. Be prepared. Seek Him in insight and wisdom. Ask Him to be courageous, to speak the truth. The enemy will seek to crush you. Have faith and believe. Speaking truth is a very important thing heaven seeks.

"Whoever is a partner with a thief hates his own life; He swears to tell the truth, but reveals nothing."

Proverbs 29:24 NKJV

Do not partner with evil and sin. Lies and schemes are a thief. Do not partner with such things. It's a setup to take you down. It comes in confusion and defense. It comes against. Rise up and declare, it's the truth that I shall live and tell.

"Will they not teach you, and tell you, and utter words from their heart?"

Job 8:10 NKJV

Show and tell His goodness. Tell His wondrous ways. Will you show by His love for you? Will you tell everything He has given you? Will you show and tell He has created you for more? Will you show and tell? Will you show and tell today? Show and tell. Sing His praise.

"and let us consider [thoughtfully] how we may encourage one another to love and to do good deeds,"

Hebrews 10:24 AMP

We are created to encourage one another. Encourage, cheer on, support, help one another. We are called. This world can seem lonely and dark. Don't let a day go by without encouraging another. Encourage and pray. Encourage and stay. Encourage, and let them see your love and faith.

"Therefore, comfort each other and edify one another, just as you also are doing."

Comfort and edify. Comfort, soothe, ease, relieve. Edify, enlighten, guide, better, refine. Comfort and edification. We are called and created to comfort each other. We are called and created to edify another through the wisdom of the Holy Spirit. We are called to do these things. We are called. Will you receive?

"Of all your gifts, you shall offer up every heave offering due to the Lord, from all the best of them, the consecrated part of them.'"

Numbers 18:29 NKJV

We are blessed to share the gifts given to us. Do not grow selfish. Do not keep these gifts for yourself. We are created to share these gifts given. Offering them to the Lord. We are called to share our gifts given. Are you righteous and true? Loving and giving? Are you sharing or storing?

"For I long to see you so that I may share with you some spiritual gift, to strengthen and establish you;"

Romans 1:11 AMP

By the Holy Spirit, gifts are given to each one of us who are willing to receive. We shall share these amazing gifts given. We shall share. These gifts are given to us of great faith, to establish us and strengthen us during the hardest of days. We are made to share these precious ways. Share them. These gifts are precious, rare gems. Share the gifts given within.

"So above all, guard the affections of your heart, for they affect all that you are. Pay attention to the welfare of your innermost being, for from there flows the wellspring of life."

Proverbs 4:23 TPT

Pay attention to your heart. What is flowing from your heart? Guard it and protect it. It affects all that you are. Let it be beating strongly in love and faith. Let it see the good with eyes of grace. Let it be Jesus in all the right ways. Let it be healthy and whole. Today, check your heart. Make it obey the Lord's way. Truth and love. A heart yielded in surrender and worship.

Be unoffendable and forgive. Walk in forgiveness. Whatever you have been offended by, I have been offended more, I hear Him say. Love doesn't keep a record of wrongs. Do not worship offense or unforgiveness.

Offense, wrongdoing, and insult. How many times are you offended? How many times are we called to forgive? I feel that I'm easily offended, and I hate it. I feel that I'm extra touchy. Maybe it's everything I walked through that makes me feel offended so loudly. He calls us to live an unoffendable life. If we are living offended, we are not able to fully pursue and walk in purpose. The key to being unoffendable is forgiveness.

Forgiveness, pardon, mercy, and grace. We are called to forgive like Jesus. He forgives our ugliest sins, so He asks us to forgive others of theirs. Lord forgive them, for they do not know what they are doing. Would it be easier to forgive if you believed most of the offense is due to rulers, evil, and principalities of this dark world and not the actual person? This helps me to see it's the spirit rising inside of them and it's not really about me. I hope this sets you free today.

"Then Jesus said, "Father, forgive them, for they do not know what they do." And they divided His garments and cast lots."

Luke 23:34 NKJV

If Jesus could overlook the pain and mocking on that day He was hung on the cross, how could we not do the same? How could we not forget an offense, when He was beaten, battered, and bruised and still chose to forgive and not lose? How? If He can forgive the worst of them, we should be able to do the same, as hard as it is. We can be free and forgive.

Many of us get stuck in unforgiveness. We get stuck in a rut. Some loathe and stay there. Some want to stop but can't seem to unlock. Some want to ride it out and give it time. I pray we all see that when we are stuck in unforgiveness, that the one it's really hurting is you and me. He wants us to be free, not stuck. Ask Him today to make forgiving your new way.

Forgiveness is key. It unlocks grief, insecurity, pain, and regret. Forgiveness takes place for us to live in a place of love, kindness, joy, and everlasting peace. Yes, He died to set us free and tells us to live in peace. To forgive and be forgiven. To love the unlovable. To share grace just as our loving Father gives grace. Help me, Father, to forgive with Your eyes and heart, and repent without harsh.

"bearing with one another, and forgiving one another, if anyone has a complaint against another; even as Christ forgave you, so you also must do."

Colossians 3:13 NKJV

I forgive. I forgive. I forgive. I forgive all the haters. I forgive all the naysayers. I forgive all the chatterboxes. I forgive the family and friends that never came. I forgive all the hate towards my name. I forgive them all, everyone from beginning to end. I forgive, oh Lord, how I forgive. I forgive 70x7. I forgive the worse of them. I forgive all they did to You. I forgive for what they put me through. The mocking and despair, I forgive everyone, everywhere. I forgive in the season I was in. I forgive, oh Heavenly Father. I repent.

"Then Peter came to Him and said, "Lord, how often shall my brother sin against me, and I forgive him? Up to seven times?" Jesus said to him, "I do not say to you, up to seven times, but up to seventy times seven."

Matthew 18:21–22 NKJV

Repent. Change your ways. Repent. Confess. We will sin. Our flesh is weak. Our spirit is strong. To live in purpose, we will have to repent daily. We will have to surrender. Ask for a repentant heart. This is key if we are to live for His kingdom.

"Repent [change your inner self—your old way of thinking, regret past sins, live your life in a way that proves repentance; seek God's purpose for your life], for the kingdom of heaven is at hand."

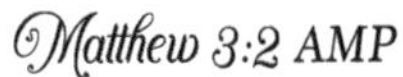

Preach, prophesy, teach, and evangelize! Go out and do these things! Preach. Speak. Advise. The kingdom of heaven is at hand. You were created to share. The kingdom of heaven is at hand. This is a very critical part of your ministry. Ask Him to share His keys!

"And as you go, preach, saying, 'The kingdom of heaven is at hand.'"

Matthew 10:7 NKJV

"And He said, "My Presence will go with you, and I will give you rest."

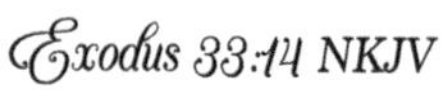

In His presence, we find rest. A rest beyond any rest. He gives us rest. He maketh us lie down in rest. Peace and rest go hand in hand. Peace and rest are a part of His plan. To do His will, you will need to learn how to rest. Live in rest, be in rest, and soak in His deep satisfying rest. If you struggle with rest, ask Him to show you His rest today.

"There remains therefore a rest for the people of God."
Hebrews 4:9 NKJV

Don't skip rest. In a world that turns so vastly, slow down and rest. It does not mean you are lazy, unworthy, or wrong. Stand up against the busy, rest, and go easy. Rest your mind. Rest your heart. Rest your body. Rest. Ask for this rest.

"Let all bitterness, and wrath, and anger, and clamor [perpetual animosity, resentment, strife, fault-finding], and slander be put away from you, along with every kind of malice [all spitefulness, verbal abuse, malevolence]."

Ephesians 4:31 AMP

Resentment can hold you up. You can't flow from His cup when resentment holds your inner being. Release the resentment and find peace. Ask Him to no longer live bitter and spiteful. Clean up your verbal ways and declare to live a new way. Resentment holds you back. Don't be the one resenting and being in lack.

"Jesus said to him, "I am the [only] Way [to God], and the [real] Truth, and the [real] Life; no one comes to the Father but through Me."

John 14:6 AMP

He is the way, the truth, and the life. He is the only way. Jesus is the only way. The only way. He is the only way. Jesus is the only way. He is truth and He is life. Spread these seeds everywhere you go, then the whole world will know!

"For you died [to this world], and your [new, real] life is hidden with Christ in God."

Colossians 3:3 AMP

He is a real living God. He is real in our lives. He is real, tangible, and good. We have died to our old self, and now live in Christ. We have given up our lives to live His. He is real, and we shall live as He sees best for us.

"I am burdened and broken by this pain. When your miracle rescue comes to me, it will lift me to the highest place."

Don't get caught up in your hurt and pain. We will all endure suffering here in the world. Don't get caught up and don't get stuck. Wrong roads are taken when we don't release and stay slain. Release it today.

We need not to fight. He won. We need not to fight in our anger, in our pain. He won that day. He won. He bore. He fought. We need to be still and know. We need not to fight. He done it all, being nailed to that tree.

"And patient endurance will refine our character, and proven character leads us back to hope."

Romans 5:4 TPT

Patient in trials will bring endurance and build Godly character. He yearns to see our character be developed. Have hope. Pray for the character of God. You were created in His image to be alike in His nature.

"Trust in the Lord completely, and do not rely on your own opinions. With all your heart rely on Him to guide you, and He will lead you in every decision you make."

Proverbs 3:5 TPT

Created for more, means to have your heart set on Him. Do not rely on your own understanding. Trust in Him to guide you, in every way, all your days. He will direct your steps when you yield in surrender and praise. Never forget your praise on those hard days. Smile, you have a God who loves and wants to see you through. Win. Conquer all things. Grin.

You were created for more.

ABOUT THE AUTHOR

I believe it's the Father, the Son, and the Holy Ghost, and everything else flows from it. I have an amazing husband, Justin, of sixteen years. I have two precious daughters that make my world go round. Addie, 14 and Liv, 9. We reside in Bourbon, MO and founded True Love Ministries. My heart is to flow from the heart of Jesus and tell the world the relationship with our Father is the most important of all.

CPSIA information can be obtained
at www.ICGtesting.com
Printed in the USA
JSHW052003151122
33258JS00003B/18